Navigating Through, Not Around, Sadness

Dr. Tarin N. Hyder

ISBN 979-8-89043-681-8 (paperback)
ISBN 979-8-89043-682-5 (digital)

Christian Faith Publishing
832 Park Avenue
Meadville, PA 16335
www.christianfaithpublishing.com

Printed in the United States of America

The book *Navigating Through, Not Around, Sadness* is given with love, hugs, and kisses.

♥ To:

♥ From:

Acknowledgments

I have so many thanks to give.

To Caleb Hyder, my amazing husband, from the depths of my soul, I thank you. I thank you for being my biggest supporter, for always believing in me, for continuously encouraging me to be my authentic self, for impromptu midday work breaks to review edited manuscripts together, and for patiently pausing your television shows late in the evening to discuss illustrations. In the truest of words, thank you for being *you*! I am who I am today because *we* navigated through this journey *together*. I love the life we've built and the journey we've been on and excitedly look forward to each new day. I love you, forever-ever.

To my children, Kiersten and Cj, my two biggest blessings, I thank you both. I thank you both for unknowingly reminding me every day of the importance of every single decision that I was making as the decisions I was making lay the foundational groundwork for some of yours. With your beautiful eyes staring at me, watching me, mimicking my behavior, and holding me accountable, I learned that my words and actions mattered more now than ever. *You taught me* that to guide you, I must lead by example, which resulted in me navigating through my own emotional healing journey. You two are the heart of this book. I love you both.

To my mom, Teresa, the constant in my life, I thank you. I thank you for always being there for me no matter the time of day or night. I thank you for loving me; for me; for your patience, especially during the big emotions of my teenage years; and for always believing in me even when I didn't believe in myself. I love you.

"Kelsee, Kelsee, I see the lightning bugs! Do you want to go outside and catch them?" Coltin asked.

"Yes! Guess what? I learned that lightning bugs' butts glow like lanterns because they are rich in a mineral called phosphorous," Kelsee explained.

"I want my butt to glow!" Coltin exclaimed.

"Me too. A glowing butt for my dance recital would be so cool! Mom told me that phosphorous is in carrots and almonds. We should have those for snack tonight," Kelsee said.

5

"I have a great idea! Let's dip our carrots in almond butter," said Coltin.

"Yum," said Kelsee.

"Oh *nooooo*! My bug vacuum!" Coltin exclaimed while grabbing his bug vacuum and running inside to show his mom.

"*Mom, Mom, Mom*, my bug vacuum is broken," he said.
"Coltin, let me take a look at it to see if we can fix it," Mom said.
"Buddy, I am sorry. You are right. Your bug vacuum is broken."

"My bug vacuum is my favorite toy," he said.
"Coltin, to me, it feels like you are feeling the emotion sadness. Do you feel sad?" Mom asked.
"Yes, I feel very sad," Coltin responded.

"It is a normal and healthy response to feel sad when our favorite toys break. Together, let's take all the time that you need to sit with sadness, and when you're ready, let's choose a tool from our toolbox to process and release sadness," Mom said.

"Mom, it is time. I am ready to let go of sadness," said Coltin.
"Which tool from our toolbox would you like to use to assist in processing and releasing sadness?" Mom asked.
"Hyder's 5-Step Protocol," Coltin responded.

"That is one of my favorite tools too buddy. With the Hyder's 5-Step Protocol, we begin by stating and validating how you feel. How do you feel?" Mom asked.

"I feel sad," Coltin said.

"When you're ready, repeat after me: 'I feel sad, and it is okay,'" Mom said.

"I feel sad, and it is okay," Coltin repeated.

"With the next step, we want to identify what is causing you to feel sad. Why do you feel sad?" Mom asked.

"I feel sad because my favorite toy bug vacuum broke," Coltin answered.

16

"When you're ready, repeat after me: 'My favorite bug vacuum breaking triggered my feelings of sadness, and it is okay,'" said Mom.

"My favorite bug vacuum breaking triggered my feelings of sadness, and it is okay," said Coltin.

"When we are having uncomfortable emotions, if we close our eyes, and feel our body, we will be able to find the spot where the emotion is hiding. Think of it like the game hide and go seek. When you're ready, gently close your eyes and feel your body. Where is sadness hiding?" Mom asked.

"Sadness is hiding in my heart," Coltin said.

"When you're ready, repeat after me: 'Sadness is hiding in my heart, and it is okay,'" Mom said.

"Sadness is hiding in my heart, and it is okay," Coltin repeated.

"The next step is describing the physical sensations that the emotion sadness is creating. We now know that sadness is hiding in your heart, but what does sadness physically feel like?" Mom asked.

"My heart feels broken," Coltin answered.

"When you're ready, repeat after me: 'Sadness to me feels like my heart is broken, and it is okay,'" Mom said.

"Sadness to me feels like my heart is broken, and it is okay," Coltin repeated.

"Coltin, you are always in control of your emotions even when it doesn't feel like it. You get to decide whether you will navigate through them or around them. Today, you courageously chose to navigate through them. Now, it's time for the final step. You get to decide how you're going to respond to the emotion sadness. How do you want to respond to the sadness that you are feeling?" Mom asked.

"I want to heal my broken heart with a Band-Aid," answered Coltin.

"Would you like me to join you, or would you like to go pick out your favorite Band-Aid by yourself?" Mom asked.

"I want you to join me," Coltin said.

23

"How does your heart feel now?" Mom asked.

"My broken heart is now whole," Coltin answered.

"Buddy, you just did the bravest thing of all. You honored your symptoms of sadness by sitting with them, finding them, feeling them, processing them, and releasing them. I am so proud of you! I love you!" Mom said.

"I love you too," Coltin said.

With the assistance of the Hyder's 5-Step Protocol, you are

1. acknowledging and honoring how you feel,
2. identifying your triggers,
3. consciously connecting to your body,
4. dissolving charged emotions, and
5. empowering yourself.

The Hyder's 5-Step Protocol

Step 1: "I feel _____, and it is okay."
Name of emotion

Step 2: "_____ triggered my feelings of _____,
Trigger   Name of emotion

and it is okay."

Step 3: "_____ is hiding in my _____,
Name of emotion   Body location

and it is okay."

Step 4: "_____ to me feels like _____,
Name of emotion   Physical sensation(s)

and it is okay."

Step 5: "I choose to respond to _____ by _____."
Name of emotion   Response

About the Author

Tarin N. Hyder is a daughter of God, a wife, a mom, a Board-Certified Traditional Naturopathic Doctor, a certified GAPS (Gut & Psychology Syndrome) Practitioner, a PSYCH-K Facilitator, and a Reiki Practitioner. Together, she and her husband Caleb are proud owners of Nature's Gateway, LLC, a holistic wellness center located in Hartland, Michigan. In addition to seeing clients in her practice, she is a teacher and counselor at the Warda Academy in Fenton, Michigan.

Tarin loves spending time with her husband, daughter Kiersten, son Cj, and mom Teresa. She enjoys learning, attending educational conferences, reading, writing, and making magic in the kitchen.

www.ingramcontent.com/pod-product-compliance
Lightning Source LLC
LaVergne TN
LVHW072345181224
799473LV00048B/1679